A RECORD BOOK ABOUT THE TURN OF THE
MILLENNIUM

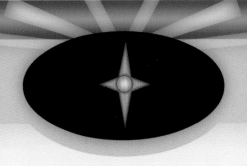

©1999 Havoc Publishing
ISBN 1-57977-143-2

Published and created by Havoc Publishing
San Diego, California

First Printing, January 1999

Printed in China

Please write to us for more information on our
Havoc Publishing Record Books and Products.

HAVOC PUBLISHING
6330 Nancy Ridge Drive, Suite 104
San Diego, California 92121

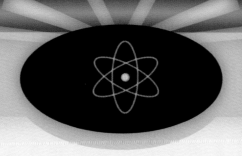

A RECORD BOOK ABOUT THE TURN OF THE
MILLENNIUM

A Record Book For

_____

CONTENTS

CONTENTS

TIMELINE
1999

Describe 1999's most significant events and record on timeline below

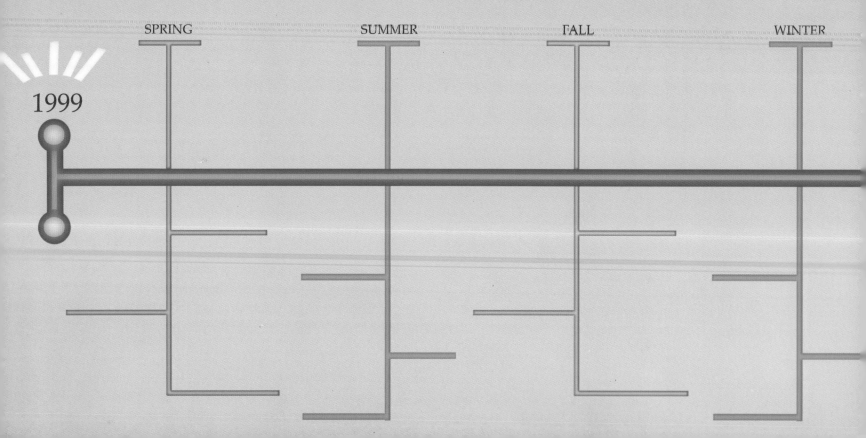

SPRING   SUMMER   FALL   WINTER

1999

Describe 2000's most significant events and record on timeline below

_____
_____
_____
_____
_____
_____
_____
_____
_____
_____
_____
_____
_____

TIMELINE
2000

SPRING   SUMMER   FALL   WINTER

2001

This year's top international news

NEWS
1999

National occurrences this year

Local developments during 1999

NEWS
2000

This year's top international news

_____

_____

_____

_____

_____

_____

_____

_____

_____

_____

National occurrences this year

_____

_____

_____

_____

_____

_____

Local developments during 2000

_____

_____

_____

_____

_____

POLITICS
1999

Political topics this year:

International _____

_____

_____

National _____

_____

Local _____

_____

Current political leaders:

International _____

_____

National _____

_____

Local _____

_____

This year's scandals _____

_____

_____

Political topics this year:

International _____

_____

_____

National _____

_____

Local _____

_____

POLITICS 2000

Current political leaders:

International _____

_____

National _____

_____

Local _____

_____

This year's scandals _____

_____

_____

_____

_____

NEWSPAPER CLIPPINGS

(Place 1999 Clippings Here)

NEWSPAPER CLIPPINGS

(Place 2000 Clippings Here)

1999's popular music stars _____

_____

_____

_____

Favorite songs of this year _____

_____

_____

_____

_____

Who / what won at the music awards _____

_____

_____

MUSIC
1999

MUSIC
2000

2000's popular music stars

_____

_____

_____

Favorite songs of this year

_____

_____

_____

_____

Who/what won at the music awards

_____

_____

MOVIES
1999

This year's popular movie stars

Favorite movies of 1999

Who/what won at the movie awards this year

This year's popular movie stars

Favorite movies of 2000

Who/what won at the movie awards this year

MOVIES
2000

(Place 1999 Memorabilia Here)

(Place 2000 Memorabilia Here)

Popular radio personalities this year _____

_____

_____

_____

RADIO
1999

This year's favorite radio talk shows _____

_____

_____

Favorite radio stations _____

_____

_____

_____

RADIO
2000

Popular radio personalities this year

_____

_____

_____

_____

This year's favorite radio talk shows _____

_____

_____

_____

Favorite radio stations _____

_____

_____

_____

_____

T.V.
1999

⭐

1999's popular television shows _____

_____

_____

_____

_____

_____

Hottest new shows _____

_____

_____

_____

_____

This year's favorite television stars _____

_____

_____

_____

Who/what won at the awards _____

_____

_____

_____

_____

2000's popular television shows _____

_____

_____

_____

_____

_____

_____

Hottest new shows _____

_____

_____

_____

_____

T.V.
2000

This year's favorite television stars _____

_____

_____

_____

_____

Who/what won at the awards _____

_____

_____

_____

_____

_____

_____

PHOTOGRAPHS

(Place 1999 Photographs Here)

PHOTOGRAPHS

(Place 2000 Photographs Here)

This year's popular writers

New books on the best-seller list

IN
WRITING
1999

Favorite magazines this year

Favorite novels and articles of 1999

IN
WRITING
2000

This year's popular writers

_____
_____
_____
_____
_____
_____

New books on the best-seller list

_____
_____
_____
_____
_____
_____

avorite magazines this year

_____
_____
_____
_____

avorite novels and articles of 2000

_____
_____
_____
_____
_____

MEMORABILIA

(Place 1999 Memorabilia Here)

MEMORABILIA

(Place 2000 Memorabilia Here)

SPORTS
1999

Which team won the 1999 championship in:

Football

_____

Baseball

_____

Basketball

_____

Hockey

_____

Other favorite sports

_____

_____

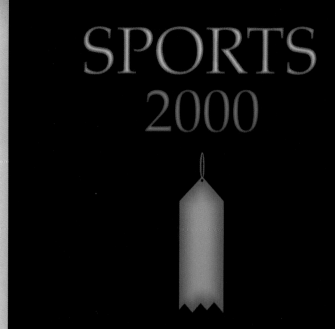

SPORTS 2000

Which team won the 2000 championship in:

Football _____

_____

Baseball _____

_____

Basketball _____

_____

Hockey _____

_____

Other favorite sports _____

_____

SPORTS MEMORABILIA

(Place Memorabilia Here)

2000

OLYMPICS

Medals won in the following events:

Gymnastics _____

Diving _____

Track and Field _____

Swimming _____

Soccer _____

Water Polo _____

Boxing _____

Weightlifting _____

Wrestling _____

Cycling _____

Tennis _____

Other event _____

Other event _____

Other event _____

Other event _____

This year's clothing trends _____

_____

_____

New automobiles on the road _____

_____

Which cuisines are popular _____

_____

_____

Activities that are trendy _____

_____

_____

1999's travel destinations _____

_____

_____

TRENDS
1999

This year's trendy sayings _____

_____

_____

TRENDS
2000

This year's clothing trends _____
_____
_____

New automobiles on the road _____
_____

Which cuisines are popular _____
_____
_____

Activities that are trendy _____
_____
_____

This year's trendy sayings _____
_____
_____

2000's travel destinations _____

PERSONAL FASHIONS

(Place Clippings/Photographs Here)

PERSONAL FASHIONS

(Place Clippings/Photographs Here)

FAMILY AND FRIENDS

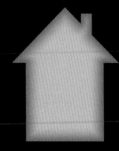

Special events that happened with family and friends:

Date _____ Event _____

Notes _____

_____

Date _____ Event _____

Notes _____

_____

Date _____ Event _____

Notes _____

_____

Date _____ Event _____

Notes _____

_____

Date _____ Event _____

Notes _____

_____

Date _____ Event _____

Notes _____

_____

Date _____ Event _____

Notes _____

_____

Date _____ Event _____

Notes _____

_____

Date _____ Event _____

Notes _____

_____

Date _____ Event _____

Notes _____

_____

Date _____ Event _____

Notes _____

_____

Date _____ Event _____

Notes _____

_____

Date _____ Event _____

Notes _____

_____

PHOTOGRAPHS

(Place 1999 Photographs Here)

PHOTOGRAPHS

(Place 2000 Photographs Here)

COST OF LIVING

Costs of the following:

Average home _____

Education _____

Automobiles _____

Computer _____

Plane ticket _____

Grocery bill _____

Electronics _____

Clothing _____

Athletic shoes _____

Haircut _____

Compact disc _____

Gallon of gas _____

Movie ticket _____

Gallon of milk _____

Magazine _____

Newspaper _____

Video rental _____

Cup of coffee _____

Postage stamp _____

The greatest increases in the cost of living ————————————————————————————————

———

———

———

———

———

———

———

The greatest decreases in the cost of living ————————————————————————————————

———

———

———

———

———

PERSONAL SIDE

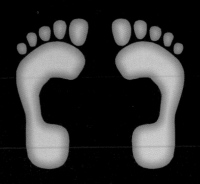

Favorite hobbies and activities_____

_____

_____

_____

Personal interests_____

_____

_____

_____

Clubs and organizations_____

_____

_____

_____

Personal accomplishments

Greatest lessons learned

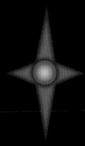

DAYS TO REMEMBER
1999

Memorable days in the spring

Summer days to remember

Favorite moments in the fall

Winter's special occasions

DAYS TO REMEMBER
2000

Memorable days in the spring _____

_____

_____

_____

_____

Summer days to remember _____

_____

_____

_____

_____

Favorite moments in the fall _____

_____

_____

_____

_____

Winter's special occasions _____

_____

_____

_____

MEMORABILIA

(Place 1999 Memorabilia Here)

MEMORABILIA

(Place 2000 Memorabilia Here)

TECHNOLOGY
1999

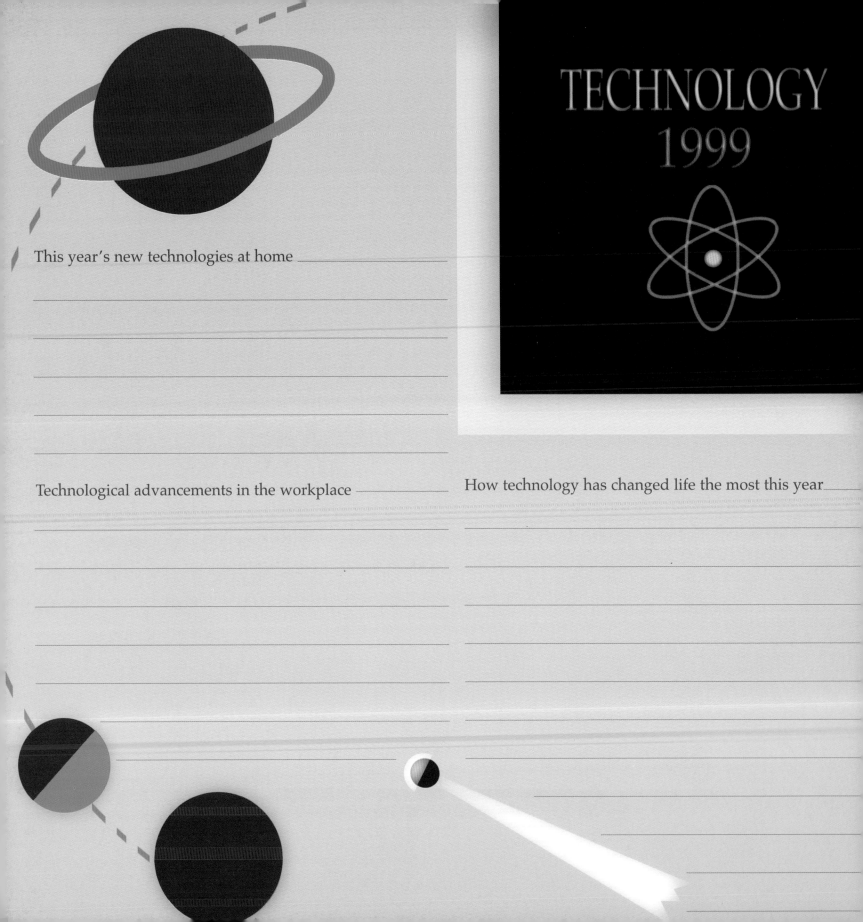

This year's new technologies at home

Technological advancements in the workplace

How technology has changed life the most this year

TECHNOLOGY
2000

This year's new technologies at home _____

_____

_____

_____

_____

_____

How technology has changed life the most this year _____

_____

_____

_____

_____

_____

_____

_____

Technological advancements in the workplace _____

_____

_____

_____

_____

_____

_____

INTERNET

Best e-mail jokes _____

_____

_____

_____

_____

_____

_____

_____

_____

Favorite websites:

Website: _____ *http:* _____

Website: _____ *http:* _____

Website: _____ *http:* _____

Website: _____ *http:* _____

Website: _____ *http:* _____

Website: _____ *http:* _____

Website: _____ *http:* _____

Website: _____ *http:* _____

Personal uses of the internet: _____

Individuals communicated with using e-mail _____

_____

_____

_____

Changes the internet has made to daily life _____

_____

_____

_____

Predictions of the internet's role in the future _____

_____

_____

_____

_____

_____

Strangest chat room conversation _____

_____

_____

_____

_____

_____

_____

_____

Best conversation in a chat room _____

_____

_____

_____

_____

_____

_____

_____

Preparations made before the conversion

_____

_____

_____

_____

_____

Supplies acquired _____

_____

_____

Expectations of the conversion _____

_____

_____

_____

_____

THE
CONVERSION
1999

?

1 0 0 1 0 0 1 0 1 0 1 0 0 1 0 0 1 0 1 1 1 0
0 0 1 0 0 1 0 1 0 0 1 0 0 1 0 1 0 1 1 1 0 1
1 0 0 1 0 0 1 0 1 0 0 1 0 0 1 0 1 0 1 1 1 0
0 0 1 0 0 1 0 1 0 0 1 0 0 1 0 1 0 1 1 1 0 1

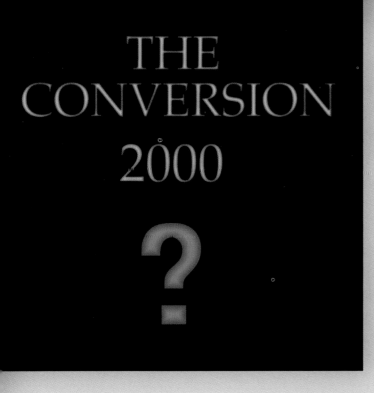

THE CONVERSION 2000 ?

What actually happened

_____

_____

_____

_____

_____

_____

_____

_____

What were the effects

_____

_____

_____

0 0 1 0 0 1 0 1 0 1 0 0 1 0 0 1 0 1 0 1 1 1 0 1
0 1 0 0 1 0 1 0 1 0 0 1 0 0 1 0 1 1 1 1 0 1 0
0 0 1 0 0 1 0 1 0 0 1 0 0 1 0 1 0 1 1 1 0 1
0 1 0 0 1 0 1 0 0 1 0 0 1 0 1 1 1 1 0 1 0

PHOTOGRAPHS

(Place 1999 Photographs Here)

PHOTOGRAPHS

(Place 2000 Photographs Here)

NEW
YEARS
1999

New Year's eve was spent _____

_____

_____

_____

_____

_____

New Year's day was spent _____

_____

_____

_____

_____

NEW YEARS 2000

New Year's eve was spent _____

_____

_____

_____

_____

_____

New Year's day was spent _____

_____

_____

_____

_____

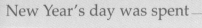

PHOTOGRAPHS

(Place 1999 Photographs Here)

PHOTOGRAPHS

(Place 2000 Photographs Here)

GOALS
1999

Goals reached this year

_____

_____

_____

_____

_____

_____

Goals set for next year

_____

_____

_____

_____

_____

GOALS
2000

Goals reached this year

Goals set for next year